Decorating with

SILK FLOWERS

Decorating With Silk Flowers
First published in Australia in 2000 by Kangaroo Press
An imprint of Simon & Schuster (Australia) Pty Limited
Suite 2, Lower Ground Floor
14-16 Suakin Street, Pymble NSW 2073

A CBS Company
Sydney New York London Toronto

National Library of Australia
Cataloguing-in-Publication data

Miles, Deborah.
    Decorating with silk flowers.

    ISBN 978 0 7318 0783 3

    1. Silk flower arrangement. 2. Silk flowers. I. Title.

745.92

Cover Design: Karen Young
Design: Vivien Valk Design
Photography: Bob Williamson, TTK Photographics

Set in Sabon 9pt/11pt
Printed in China through Colorcraft Ltd., Hong Kong

10 9 8 7 6 5 4

Decorating with
SILK FLOWERS

DEBORAH MILES

Kangaroo Press

When you set out to create a floral arrangement you must keep in mind the setting, the container being used, the colour and texture of the flowers, and the size and shape of the arrangement, if the final effect is to be striking and well balanced. Your choice of floral colours will reflect your personal taste. Experimenting is half the fun and you may be pleasantly surprised, as in the mixing here of tulips, water lilies, gourds and pods with tiger lilies.

Acknowledgments

A special thank you to Barbara Slatyer for her creative and stylistic input during the photography.

My thanks also to the following people for providing their support with time and materials as well as opening the doors of their establishments for photographic backdrops:
Ruth and Steve Logan of Mananga Homestead B & B, Berry
Barbara and Harvey Slatyer of Haven and Space Homewares, Berry
Julieann and Robert Salmon of Salmon & Co. Restaurant, Berry
Beth and Robert Packer of Pottering Around, Berry
Lyn Havilah of Tindilah Pottery, Berry

Contents

Introduction

Without many of us realising it, flowers play a very important part in our lives. The extension of our gardens, which can give so much pleasure, into our homes adds to the charm and welcome when we enter a house. Flowers, like music, enrich our lives. For different occasions and for different reasons, from a bouquet for a bride to a simple yet elegant swag to welcome a guest to a bedroom, flowers can add the finishing touch.

Today's busier lifestyle, however, doesn't always allow us the time to pay regular attention to the smaller finishing details in our homes. With the abundance and beauty of the deceptively real silk flowers now available, it is quite easy to create an arrangement that is going to be simple to maintain and look good for quite some time.

The mixing of silk flowers with fresh flowers is also becoming increasingly popular, especially in the corporate sector and in restaurants, places of high traffic density and intense lighting. Such a mixture not only provides value for money but the silk flowers also tend to keep the arrangement looking good for longer, even though the fresh flowers may be ready to be replaced.

More and more people are discovering the joy of floral arranging, whether with silk or fresh flowers. I like to keep my arrangements uncluttered, with a contemporary, classic or cottage feel that would be at home in just about any setting. Be aware of the style of arrangement that will best suit a particular position to create the desired feel or impact.

I really enjoy tailoring designs for a client's home. Visiting a home before I start putting an arrangement together helps greatly with inspiration and colour choice. If I can't get there I ask many detailed questions to allow me to envisage what they are describing. Seeing the delight on clients' faces when they receive their arrangement is the biggest thrill. So far I've never had anyone in tears of disappointment.

Silk flowers can bring the garden permanently indoors, whether in a casual, bright and cheerful arrangement such as the posy of gerberas or a more formal arrangement such as the crimson and white roses with blue gum leaves.

Colour themes

For creative outdoor lighting, candles could be added to the pots of flowers attached to an interesting frame such as this. Ensure the frame is out of the breeze, however, as you do not want the flowers to catch alight.

This book is divided into colour sections to make it easier to demonstrate the instant effect a bright or subtle touch of floral decor can have on your home. Colour fashions come and go—sometimes pale and pretty is the rage, sometimes bold and bright. I have included both detailed instructions for arrangements, and inspirational photographs, in five major colour groups, to suit a variety of colour schemes and decorating styles. For example, many home decorators are now exploring the ranges of paint and furnishing colours available in the retro revival of colours which are intense and clear. See the section 'Bright and bold' for examples of arrangements which can stand alone or contrast with each other to enliven surroundings of bold colour and tones of electric lime and blue, bright red, yellow and orange.

Other arrangements feature a monochromatic colour scheme, achieved by the use of a single colour. The chosen colour, however, can vary in shade, which will create depth in the arrangement. Monochromatic colours are easy to use and create a simple background for other features.

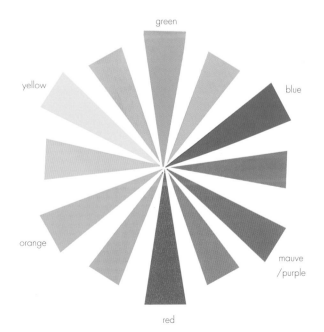

The colour wheel

The colour wheel

Other colour themes—harmonious, complementary or triadic—can be chosen with the help of a colour wheel.

Harmonious schemes involve the choice of two shades directly to the left or right of the chosen colour on the wheel. Harmonious colours are best suited for creating a flowing effect.

Complementary schemes provide a strong contrast between colours. The complementary colour is found directly opposite the chosen colour on the wheel.

The triad scheme is achieved by choosing three colours that are equidistant on the wheel. An example would be blue, red and yellow. The chosen colours should complement the chosen container—alternatively, the container could provide the third colour with two chosen floral colours.

For any arrangement following these colour schemes greenery will help provide background and definition. However, an arrangement of greenery alone looks terrific for a monochromatic scheme, as there is a fantastic abundance of artificial greenery available in all shades and leaf shapes.

Tools of the Trade

A.

B.

C.

The freelance or hobby floral artist will find sufficient basic equipment around the house—pliers, secateurs, scissors, knife and glue, preferably a hot or cold glue gun and refill sticks. Other supplies—dry Oasis, wires (from 18 gauge, which is very heavy, through to 24 gauge, which is very fine), stem wrap, Oasis spikes and moss—can be obtained cheaply from florists or craft shop outlets.

Containers and wreath bases

Containers and wreath bases are many and varied in style and can add a whole new dimension to a particular arrangement. Basically, anything that has a slight dip or hole can contain flowers—even a paper bag! Letting your imagination run wild can provide some surprising results.

Wreath bases can be bought ready-made, created out of plaited raffia or, for the adventurous, made from supple willow twigs cut straight from the tree, or vine branches, woven together.

A. *Containers for formal arrangements come in many shapes and sizes.*

B. *Basketry and tinware provide starting points for many informal and country-style arrangements.*

C. *Wreath bases can be formal and tidy, intended to be completely hidden by flowers and greenery, or informal and twiggy, with the twigs being part of the overall effect.*

Wiring and taping

Wiring stems adds stability as well as providing extra length when required. To create extra length, stems cut from other silk flowers can be wired together. Create a hook at one end of the wire, place against the flower stems, then wrap the long end of the wire around the stems. The end result is shown in the photo.

Taping with florist tape takes a bit of practice. I work from left to right (if you are left-handed, reverse the direction), placing the end of the tape on the stem where the wiring begins. Twist the stem, overlapping the tape onto itself. Following the steps in the photos, hold the start of the taping with the left thumb and twist the flower stem, at the same time stretching the tape along the stem with your right hand until it covers the length of the stem. Stretch the tape to break it off.

Florist's wire in different gauges, wired flowers and leaves and a roll of stem tape.

Step 1: Wired stem ready for taping.

Step 2: Starting the taping.

Step 3: Twisting the stem and taping down the support wire.

Ribbon bow

Estimate the length of ribbon you need to make a bow with the number of loops you require, and add several centimetres more for good measure. Pinching ribbon between thumb and forefinger, turn a length of ribbon back on itself to create the desired sized loop. Repeat this two or four times to create the size bow you desire. Fuller, more luxuriant bows can be created by using wider ribbon or a greater number of loops. Hook a length of wire over the centre of the bow, wrap the leg of ribbon from the last loop around the wire and tug gently. This hides the wire at the front of the bow. Twist wire together at back of bow to secure. Cut bow legs to desired length.

Step 1: Starting the bow.

Step 2: Gathered bow ready to secure.

Step 3: Making a loop to conceal the wire.

Step 4: Completed bow.

White, Cream & Green

Camellias, lisianthus
and zinnias combine with fern,
amaranthus and ivy to
create a formal and harmonious
arrangement.

Magnolia swag

50 CM (20 IN) SWAG BASE

MAGNOLIA BUSH OR
3 SINGLE HEADS AND LEAVES

GOLD GUM

RED BRIDAL GUM

SEA-LAVENDER

1 M (39 IN) WIRE-EDGED RIBBON

WIRE

PLIERS

GLUE

SCISSORS

Turn swag to face desired direction. Create a hanging loop by taking a strand of wire through the centre back of the swag, near the top.

Remove leaves from the magnolia stem and glue them along the swag base, positioning the larger leaves in the centre with the smaller leaves along the arms of the swag.

Cut the magnolia heads, leaving each with a short stem, and glue into swag base. Position evenly.

Glue gold gum around the magnolias and along swag arms. Repeat with red bridal gum and sea-lavender, ensuring an even distribution.

Create two loops of ribbon, wire the ends, and glue under foliage at ends of swag arms.

*A bowl of gardenias which can be enjoyed
all year round, indoors or outdoors.*

Celebration basket

This basket is an ideal gift to welcome the arrival of a
baby or to say 'Get well'.

OASIS

3 LILIES

3 LILY BUDS

SILK FERN STEMS

DRIED TEA-TREE

BLUE GUM

RED BRIDAL GUM

RIBBON

KNIFE

GLUE

BASKET

WIRE

PLIERS

SCISSORS

This arrangement is to be viewed from the front.

Cut Oasis to the required shape, then glue in position
towards the back of the basket. Secure the Oasis with wire
pins through the bottom of the basket.

Starting with the blue gum, define the outline of the
arrangement. Repeat with the bridal gum, fern stems and tea-
tree, filling in the gaps.

Cut the stems of the lilies and the lily buds with pliers and
position in triangular formation.

NB: Make the lily stems longer than the bud stems to allow
the lilies to sit out from the foliage.

Create a bow (see page 9) and insert to complete the
arrangement.

A variation on the gift or presentation basket is to arrange the
flowers to one side of the basket or container, leaving room to
include a gift. Baskets can be created for any occasion—
house-warming, anniversary, new job, friendship—you can
use any excuse to give a gift. Gifts can range from theatre
tickets to homewares, lingerie, candles, gardening utensils—
the more creative the thought the more memorable the gift.
Add a hand-made card and the basket is complete.

*Gift baskets of silk flowers can provide happy
memories long after the event has passed.*

Elegance: formal design

The arrangement opposite (A) would be perfect to adorn any formal affair or as a show-piece in your home.

Changing the colour tones would give this arrangement a whole new look, making it suitable for many different locations.

Remember, one of the best things about using silk flowers is the ease of changing the colours of an arrangement.

OASIS

MOSS

CREAM OR GOLD CONTAINER

1 STEM BELL-FLOWER

2 STEMS QUEEN ANNE'S LACE

FERN LEAVES

1 STEM LISIANTHUS

2 LILY STEMS

2 STEMS SNOW IN SUMMER

2 STEMS DOGWOOD

1 GARDENIA BUSH

TWIG STEMS

KNIFE

PLIERS

WIRE

COPPER WIRE OR GOLD RIBBON

SCISSORS

Cut Oasis to fit container snugly. Cover with moss. Starting at the back left corner of container stagger the height of the flowers towards the front right corner and extend them past the container. This creates the balance of the design. The bell-flower, Queen Anne's lace and fern leaves create the design outline. The remainder of the flowers simply fill out the design—cut the stems to the required length and bend them if necessary. (Remember to allow an extra 6 or 7 cm/2"–3" to compensate for the depth of the container.) Cut twig stems into short lengths and wire. Wrap copper wire around silver wire to conceal it, or use bows of gold ribbon to hide silver wiring if copper wire is not available. Insert into the arrangement.

B. *Use left-over flowers from large arrangements to form a collection of little arrangements in like tones.*

C. *The simplicity of white and cream creates a style of elegance and purity.*

D. *White lilies give this topiary a classic look that will appear striking in any situation.*

A

B

C

D

Hues of Blue

An eye-catching wreath is
created using cream roses and
clustered blue hydrangea flowers.
This would be perfect as a house-
warming gift in any colour.

Blue moon swag

75 CM (30 IN) CRESCENT-SHAPED
SWAG BASE

BLUE GUM

7 BLUE ROSES

7 CREAM ROSES

2 M (2 YDS 8 IN) BLUE RIBBON

DRY HYDRANGEA

SEA-LAVENDER

WIRE

PLIERS

GLUE

SCISSORS

Turn swag to face desired direction. Create a hanging loop by taking a strand of wire through the centre back of the swag, near the top.

Cut blue gum into short lengths and glue into swag base. Starting from the outer arms of the swag, layer the lengths up towards the centre of swag. Remember to glue the pieces pointing out and over the edges of the swag to create a rambling look.

Cut the rose stems to varying lengths with the pliers.

Hint: Place roses loose in their positions to ensure the creation of a balanced look before gluing in place.

Glue the blue roses in place first, one at the end of each swag arm, and moving towards the centre. Repeat with the cream roses.

Make a ribbon bow and position it at the centre, glue, then weave long ribbon arms through the roses and foliage.

Cut a few small stems of hydrangea and glue into gaps in the foliage in the centre of the swag. Repeat with sea-lavender, being more generous with its distribution throughout the arrangement.

Burgundy or pink roses could be substituted in this arrangement to suit a different decor.

Floral swags provide a touch of detail that helps to make a house a home.

Iris and rose posy

LARGE BUNCH CREAM CABBAGE
ROSES OR SIMILAR

7 BLUE IRIS

SILK WHEAT

BLUE GUM

SPEAR GRASS

2 M (2 YDS 8 IN) STRING BEADS

6 LARGE MAGNOLIA OR
HYDRANGEA LEAVES

2 M (2 YDS 8 IN) RIBBON

PLIERS

WIRES

STEM TAPE (SEE PAGE 9)

SCISSORS

Cut the stems of the roses, iris and wheat to approximately 15 cm (6").

Cut the blue gum to the same length, stripping some of the lower leaves from the stems.

Cut the spear grass to 20 cm (8") lengths.

Wire all flower stems and cover with stem tape.

Cut beading into 20 cm (8") lengths, form each length into a loop, wire, and cover wire with stem tape.

To make the bouquet, start with an iris as the centre-point, then gradually add roses, blue gum, wheat, spear grass and wired beads. Lay flower stems across one another from left to right, turning the bouquet constantly to ensure a balanced look and even distribution of flowers. As the bouquet increases in volume, gently bend the outer flowers out to create a rounded dome shape. Finish off with the large magnolia or hydrangea leaves at the base of the bouquet.

To secure the bouquet, make a fairly firm wrap of spool or continuous wire around the top of the massed stems, as shown in the photo. Cut stem ends evenly. Tie ribbon over the wire securing the posy and complete with a bow. Cut ribbon tails to desired length.

Table centrepiece

A simple table centrepiece made from just a few of the flowers used in the bouquet
can add a delightful finishing touch.

OASIS

SMALL URN

TAPER CANDLE, PREFERABLY DRIPLESS

MOSS

LONG STEM OF IVY

3 ROSES

3 IRIS

RIBBON

KNIFE

PLIERS

SCISSORS

Cut the Oasis to fit the urn, then cut a well in the centre of the Oasis to hold the candle. The well should be a tight fit to ensure the candle does not topple over. Cover the top of the urn and the Oasis with moss. Cut the ivy into two unequal lengths and insert into the Oasis on each side of the urn.

Cut off most of the rose and iris stems, leaving just a short piece to insert into the Oasis. Alternate the rose and iris heads around the Oasis. Create 2 small bows and insert on either side of the arrangement, then add the candle in the centre to finish.

Simplicity and elegance
go hand-in-hand

Cottage garden bowl

Spring flowers can be enjoyed in the home all year round

with this casual pot of blooms.

A.

B.

OASIS BRICK

BOWL OR VASE WITH REASONABLY WIDE OPENING

OASIS SPIKE

SHORT STEM SPEAR GRASS

3 DAISY STEMS

3 CORNFLOWER STEMS

3 FREESIA STEMS, LAVENDER

1 PERUVIAN LILY STEM, YELLOW

2 CROCOSMIA STEMS, DUSTY PINK

KNIFE AND PLIERS

OASIS FIX OR BLU-TAK

I have based this arrangement in a beautiful Chinese ginger jar.

Cut the Oasis to fit snugly in the bowl or vase you have chosen. Attach the Oasis spike with Oasis fix or Blu-Tak to the base of the vase. Push the Oasis on to the spike to secure it in the container. (Because of the rounded sides of the jar and the lack of weight in the flowers to hold them in position, anything not secured will slide up the sides of the jar and dislodge itself. The combination of Oasis spike and Oasis fix or Blu-Tak means the container is not subjected to the shock of hot glue, and is much safer for antique containers.)

Insert spear grass in centre of Oasis. Cut the daisy stems to varying lengths and distribute around the bowl, ensuring that some of the heads extend beyond the bowl edge. The same principle applies to all the other flowers in this arrangement— the cornflowers, freesias, Peruvian lily and crocosmia.

Pull some of the arms of the spear grass through the flowers to create movement and soften the outline of the flowers.

A. *Flowers glued around the edge of a bowl create a delightful display. The bowl can be filled with potpourri, pine cones, chocolates, body products or, as in this case, a very large dripless candle.*

B. *Versatile blues, mauves and lilacs are cool and calming in softer tones, or can create a dynamic contrast in their stronger tones.*

In the Red

A dramatic bowl of roses
and gerberas with a lace cloth
creates on old-fashioned feel.
Add gold ribbon or berries for
a quick Christmas display.

Kitchen spice wreath

30 CM (12 IN) WREATH BASE

3 BERRY PICKS

CINNAMON STICKS

3 X 20 CM (8 IN) LENGTHS OF
GREEN CHECK RIBBON OR FABRIC

BLUE GUM

RAFFIA

WIRE

GLUE

PLIERS

SCISSORS

Turn the wreath to face desired direction. Create a hanging loop by taking a strand of wire through the centre back of the wreath, near the top.

Glue the three berry picks in a triangular formation into the wreath. Splay out the leaves.

Divide the lengths of cinnamon into three groups, and hold them together with a dab of glue at the centre.

Thread a length of ribbon or fabric through the wreath between an upper pair of berry picks. Glue a cinnamon bundle in place over the ribbon, and tie the ribbon tails around the bundle. Repeat with a second cinnamon bundle.

Cut blue gum into varying lengths and glue in and around the berry picks. Allow longer lengths of gum to slightly overlap the two cinnamon bundles.

Create a bow from the raffia and glue into centre base of the wreath. Tie the third bundle of cinnamon on top of the raffia bow with a third length of ribbon or fabric.

Wheat, and almonds in the shell, can be added to this wreath for greater variety, as can purple larkspur for dramatic contrast in colouring.

Cinnamon, spice and all things nice combine to create a warm country kitchen wreath.

My Valentine: pot of roses

OASIS

TERRACOTTA POT

6 SUEDE ROSE STEMS

6 BUXUS PICKS

RIBBON

KNIFE

PLIERS

GLUE

SCISSORS

Trim Oasis to fit snugly in pot.

Using pliers, cut the rose stems to desired length, making the stem of the centre rose slightly longer than the others. Trim excess leaves from rose stems and put to one side.

Push the roses into the Oasis, starting with the centre rose. Arrange the other five roses evenly around the edge of the pot, angling them away from the centre rose.

Trim the buxus stems and insert between the rose stems to hide the Oasis. The extra rose leaves can be pushed in between the pot rim and the buxus and secured with glue.

Add a ribbon bow among the roses or tie a ribbon around the edge of the pot if you prefer.

This arrangement makes an ideal, inexpensive gift that will last. Roses of any colour look great in this display—don't be limited by the idea that this is only a St Valentine's Day idea.

A variation on the St Valentine's Day arrangement just described keeps the roses on their long stem to feature in a wall spray or swag. This arrangement's base is a twig branch which creates an elegant country feeling.

Mediterranean wall planter

A.

B.

Cut Oasis to fit inside planter, secure with glue.

Cut rose stems, ensuring that the longest stem, for the centre back rose, is twice the height of the planter. Insert in the Oasis, then insert the next two roses, with their stems cut a little shorter. Make the last three slightly shorter again.

Place varying lengths of grandfather's whiskers around the roses, and trail the ivy down the front of the pot, securing it in the Oasis with glue.

Cut freesia stems fairly long. (Some freesia stems have removable leaves which can be reused elsewhere.) Position freesias in front of the roses, ensuring that they spill forward over the edge of the pot.

OASIS

TERRACOTTA WALL PLANTER

4 STEMS GRANDFATHER'S WHISKERS
(CAN BE PURCHASED FRESH FROM A FLORIST AND WILL DRY EASILY IN THE ARRANGEMENT)

PALE PINK ROSEBUDS ON LONG STEMS

2 STEMS IVY

3 DOUBLE-HEADED RED FREESIA STEMS

KNIFE AND PLIERS

GLUE

A. *Wild vine wreaths sometimes need very little extra decoration, as they have an interesting look of their own with their broken outlines. A few large-headed flowers work best with such wreaths, giving a minimalist look; over-decorating with small flowers can make these wreaths look too busy.*

B. *Rich and warm, red tones bring excitement with a splash of colour.*

Pinks & Pastels

A dainty bowl of apricot roses
ringed with green hydrangea would
make a pleasant addition to any room.

Branching out

2 X 60 CM (24 IN) VINE BRANCHES

BLUE GUM

1 BRANCH OF CAMELLIA LEAF

1 BUNCH DUSTY PINK ROSES

1 BUNCH CREAM ROSES

1 M (39 IN) RIBBON

WIRE

PLIERS

GLUE

SCISSORS

Overlap the two vine branches and wire together firmly in a pleasing arrangement.

Create a hanging loop by taking a strand of wire through the centre back of the vine branches. Cut blue gum into varying lengths and glue along the vine branches.

Remove camellia leaves from stem in sections, and glue along branch between the blue gum sprays, clustering the sprays more towards the centre area where vine branches overlap.

Cut heads from rose sprays, leaving each with a short stem, and position along the vine branches, clustering any larger roses in the centre area and placing smaller flowers along branch arms. Glue roses in place.

Make a bow with at least four loops and glue into centre area. If you like you can trail long ribbon arms from the bow through the arrangement.

A. *Using either a bow wreath or a crossed vine base, arrangements to match the one just described can be made very quickly.*

B. *Positioning is important. Here the reflection of light through the leadlight door creates an interesting framework around a bow wreath decorated in mainly pastel tones. The darker red cosmos add a stronger note.*

Pretty as a picture: wall pocket

OASIS BRICK

SMALL CANE WALL PLANTER

MOSS

BLUE GUM

CAMELLIA LEAF BRANCH

WHITE TEA-TREE

2 STEMS AZARA SPRAY

6 PEACH ROSES
(OR COLOUR OF YOUR CHOICE)

RIBBON TO MATCH

KNIFE

WIRE

PLIERS

SCISSORS

Cut Oasis into a wedge, secure with glue into the pocket of the wall planter, and fix in place with wire pins through the back of the pocket. The Oasis should sit slightly higher than the front edge of the pocket.

Cover Oasis with moss.

Cut lengths of blue gum and distribute around the Oasis, ensuring they extend over the sides and front of the pocket. Repeat with camellia leaf and tea-tree.

Cut rose stems with pliers and insert in a triangular or fan pattern.

Cut azara stems with pliers and distribute evenly around the arrangement.

Finish with a wired bow of at least four loops at the front of the pocket, tucked in under the foliage.

Wall pockets can be hung from door handles, or tied to a chair, to provide the finishing touch to a room.

Gardenia and rose basket

A.

B.

OASIS BRICK

MEDIUM OR LARGE PETAL BASKET (OR BASKET OF CHOICE)

MOSS

BLUE GUM

SMALL GARDENIA BUSH OR SIMILAR

7 LARGE PINK ROSES

12 SMALL BURGUNDY ROSES

WHITE TEA-TREE

ᘛᘚ

KNIFE AND PLIERS

GLUE

WIRE

Cut Oasis to fit in centre of basket, secure with glue and fix with wire pins up through base of basket.

Cover Oasis with moss. Cut blue gum into lengths that will extend beyond the sides of the basket. Distribute evenly.

Cut gardenia bush stems into smaller sections and distribute evenly around basket. Any extra leaves can be used to fill in gaps.

Distribute the large roses evenly through the arrangement, and then place the small roses.

Fill in any gaps between the flowers with tea-tree.

B. *A terracotta saucer provides a simple base for a quick outdoor table arrangement of roses and gardenias with a fat white dripless candle.*

C. *Flower arrangements should not be thought of as rigid displays; rather they should interact with the room setting to create a personal harmonious atmosphere. A simple pot of roses and misty-blue tea-tree alongside a decorative saucer of potpourri makes a romantic statement.*

D. *Pastels mixed with deeper colour shades bring a sense of romance and indulgence.*

C

D

Bright & Bold

The vivid colours and shapes
of bird of paradise flowers,
tiger lilies and gerberas can create
an impressive display suitable
for a corporate setting.

Tropical delights

OASIS

POT

MOSS

2 LONG SPEAR LEAVES

3 SHORT SPEAR LEAVES

1 SPEARGRASS STEM

1 DRAGON FERN

1 FERN BRANCH

3 HELICONIA OR BIRD OF PARADISE SPRAYS

3 IVY STEMS

3 CALLA LILIES OR ANTHURIUMS

4 DRYANDRAS

2 PROTEAS

KNIFE

WIRE

PLIERS

GLUE

Cut and fit Oasis in pot, bringing it no higher than pot rim.

Cover top of Oasis with moss. Secure moss close to pot edge with either glue or pins created from wire.

Working in a multi-layered fashion from the back of the pot, cut and insert leaves and ferns, decreasing height towards front and extending over sides of pot.

Cut the heliconia or bird of paradise stems to three different lengths and insert. Use the offcuts from these stems in the arrangement, wrapping a length of ivy around one stem for added interest.

Around the front of the pot arrange the dryandra in a cluster to the left, the proteas in the centre and the calla lilies or anthuriums off-centre to the right, ensuring they extend over the edge.

This arrangement has more dramatic impact if it is raised off the ground on a stand.

A 'warm' welcome to any reception area or home.

Fruit and flowers

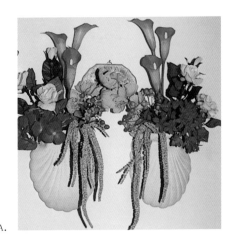

A.

DRY OASIS BRICK

15 CM (6 IN) ROUND OR SQUARE CONTAINER

3 RED/ORANGE TULIPS

1 STEM SILK WHEAT

2 LOTUS PODS

3 LONG CINNAMON STICKS

1 BERRY STEM (ANY SELECTION OF FRUIT CAN BE USED)

1 YELLOW TIGER LILY STEM

3 ORANGE DAISIES (OR GERBERAS)

1 CRIMSON WATER LILY

3 POMEGRANATES

3 GOURDS

RAFFIA

KNIFE

PLIERS

GLUE

WIRE

SCISSORS

This arrangement is created by working in a circular pattern, using blocks of colour for the most dramatic effect.

Cut Oasis to fit snugly in container and secure with glue.

Tulips and wheat are placed left and right of centre, lotus pods and cinnamon sticks next, all in layered heights.

Working around the outside, group like colours together. Any leaves on stems, cut from flower heads, can be used to fill in gaps around flower heads. Berry stems will need to be cut into multiple shorter lengths. Spare loose leaves can be pushed into Oasis under flowers to create a balanced finish.

Bundle three short lengths of cinnamon together, secure with wire. Wrap raffia around wire to hide it and push into Oasis.

This arrangement makes a terrific centrepiece for a party table. Following the same principles, you can make a fantastic variation in fresh vegetables and flowers.

A. *Antique twin wall planters with calla lilies, roses, crocus, amaranthus, agapanthus, hydrangea and hypericum berries.*

Bridal Bouquet

Rich champagne roses, lisianthus, liliums and dogwood combine in a long-lasting reminder,
for today's bride, of her special day. While ivory is still a popular choice for floral wedding colour, today's bridal
fashions allow for a great diversity of style and floral colour to complement the dresses.

A.

OASIS POSY HOLDER ('BRIDIE')

7 CM (3 IN) DRY OASIS BALL

MOSS

FLOWERS OF CHOICE

RIBBON

PLIERS

WIRE

SCISSORS

GLUE

The use of silk flowers for weddings is becoming increasingly popular as they more and more closely replicate the real thing. A silk bouquet will last a lot longer than fresh flowers (unless, of course, the fresh flowers are pressed and preserved—which can be extremely expensive).

Bridal bouquets take on many shapes—from posies, teardrops and trailing arrangements to a sheaf cradled in the arms. Bouquets should be designed to complement the bride's dress. The time spent wiring bouquets can be reduced by the use of a posy holder, especially if the flowers are all silk or are mixed with dried flowers. Remove the wet Oasis that comes with the holder and insert a dry Oasis ball.

Start by pinning moss over the ball, then create the outline of the bouquet with foliage. (Bend 6 cm of wire in half to create a V-shaped pin.)

For maximum effect cluster the flowers in blocks of colour. Flowers can be tightly and evenly arranged for a formal design, or left on longer stems of varying lengths to create a larger and less formal design. The greater the variety of flowers used the less formal the arrangement.

Finish the bouquet with a large bow, glued or tied to the top of the bridie handle and tucked slightly into the flowers.

A. *A head ring made to match
the bridal bouquet.*

Christmas

An ivy-covered wreath base
topped with berries and gold bead
garland makes for a quick and
stylish Christmas decoration.

Festive wreath

A.

B.

C.

Turn wreath to face desired direction. Make a hanging loop by taking a strand of wire through the centre back of the wreath, near the top.

Add glue to stems of fruit and Christmas picks and insert into wreath, covering it generously. The arrangement should look fairly balanced, with larger fruits positioned towards the base of the wreath. Leave a space at the centre top for the bow.

Make a bow with at least four loops and fairly long arms and glue into place.

30 CM (12 IN) VINE WREATH

MIXTURE OF VARIOUS FRUIT AND CHRISTMAS PICKS

1.5 M (1 YD 23 IN) RICH CHRISTMAS RIBBON TO MATCH

WIRE AND GLUE

PLIERS AND SCISSORS

B, C. *Oval wreath shapes and swags provide a nice variation on the standard round Christmas wreath. Colours other than the traditional red and green can also be used for Christmas decorations, especially when combined with gold.*

Table decoration

This twig branch grouped with a couple of festive candles makes a quick and
cheerful table piece, or a wonderful hanging decoration.

1.5 M (1 YD 23 IN) RICH WIRE-EDGED RIBBON

60 CM (24 IN) VINE BRANCH

1 CHRISTMAS PICK

1 BUNCH GOLD BERRIES OR SIMILAR

SCISSORS

GLUE

PLIERS

Make a bow with one long arm to trail along the branch, and
glue into place. Trim Christmas pick stems and berry stems to
3 cm (1¼ in) and glue on either side of bow. Make a wire
loop if the twig is to be hung.

*Christmas branches create an interesting
table decoration accompanied by candles.*

Candle collars

Cut ribbon to fit around candle, allowing an overlap of 1.5 cm (¾ in). Hold ribbon in place around candle, run glue along overlap and press together. The ribbon collar can be pushed down the candle as it slowly melts.

Note: Do not leave burning candles unattended.

CHRISTMAS RIBBON

2 OR MORE FAT, NON-DRIP CANDLES

SCISSORS

GLUE

Clusters of candles similarly decorated and lit create an inviting focal point in a room.

Candle wreath

A.

B.

(Although the wreath sounds rather large, by the time all the additions are in place a smaller wreath would be too tight for a fat candle.)

Wind ribbon around wreath, overlap ends and secure with glue.

Make two generous ribbon bows, gluing one over ribbon join on the wreath, the other on the opposite side.

Trim stems of picks to 3 cm (1¼") and glue picks next to the bows.

Place the non-drip candle in the centre of the wreath.

2 M (2 YDS 8 IN) CHRISTMAS RIBBON

18 CM (7 IN) WREATH

2 CHRISTMAS PICKS

FAT NON-DRIP CANDLE TO FIT INSIDE WREATH

GLUE

SCISSORS

PLIERS

B. *A buxus wreath, created from several picks, makes an unusual candle collar. Bead garlands or berries could be added to turn it into a festive wreath, or it could be teamed with festive table decorations to set the scene.*

C. *Bundles of cinnamon sticks with festive picks glued or tied to them are quick to make, while Christmas wouldn't be the same without a tree. A small topiary Christmas tree provides a pleasant change.*

Handy Hints

Take the container you are planning to use, and colour swatches matching your décor, when selecting flowers and/or fruit and greenery for a permanent arrangement, as this will make the decision-making process much easier. However, don't limit yourself by thinking that you should always try to match floral colours exactly to your interiors.

Colours which harmonise or contrast with your decor can create a delightful display. Trust your instincts and your eyes to tell you what works and what doesn't. If you are still in doubt about the flowers or arrangement style, ask for assistance from the floral supplier.

Arrange flower colours in blocks for maximum impact. One flower of each colour here and there becomes tiring to the eye, and creates the risk of boredom.

Where you integrate candles into your work, use the dripless sort for preference. These minimise the risk of wax damaging the flowers or table surfaces, and reduce fire hazard. Naked flames should never be left unattended.

When creating an arrangement avoid a too-round or too-smooth appearance. Having all flowers and foliage at the same height, for example, and/or kept within the width of the wreath or container, is uninteresting to the eye. An irregular outline adds the interest of movement, and enhances the arrangement.

Silk flower maintenance

Never spray silk flowers with hairspray—this attracts dust, makes the flowers sticky and will eventually cause discolouration. Super Surface Sealer spray, which you should be able to obtain from good craft stores, provides a protective finish for fabrics and many other materials without gloss or discolouring.

To maintain silk flowers requires little effort. A feather duster is fine for flowers fixed in place, or you can use a hair-dryer on a low setting. Silk flowers will take tougher treatment than many dried flowers, which tend to become brittle over time. Loose silks in a vase, or flower heads that can be removed from their stems, can be cleaned by placing them in a bag with uncooked rice grains. Shaking the bag will help dislodge dust from hard to reach areas of the flowers. Some silk flowers will tolerate being cleaned with a slightly damp cloth, but do not do this unless the flowers have first been dusted, as you risk rubbing in the dust and leaving dark smudges.

Cloth flowers will benefit from a product called Rubgum, which I found at the supermarket, and which may also be available at some large hardware stores. It's a dry shampoo for lampshades—a small bag of a grit-free powder that absorbs dirt. Follow the manufacturer's instructions.

Regular cleaning of your silk flowers will keep them looking as new and give them a longer life, as will keeping them out of direct sunlight. Any floral displays intended to sit outside must be placed in a covered area protected from the elements, otherwise the results of your hard work will very quickly become tatty and faded. Boxwood or buxus is one of the few artificial plants which will cope with outdoor conditions.

Suppliers

BOTANIC ART
78 QUEEN STREET
BERRY NSW 2535
02 4464 2635 (PHONE AND FAX)

FLORAL CRAFT WAREHOUSE
UNIT 3/114 STATION ROAD
SEVEN HILLS NSW 2147
02 9674 6526

SHIRE FLOWER BARN
4 TOORAK AVE
TAREN POINT NSW 2229
02 9542 0961

THE VERY THING
SHOP 1005
CARINDALE SHOPPING CENTRE
CARINDALE QLD 4152
07 3398 4426

FLORAL INTERIORS
FACTORY 1/9 PILGRIM COURT
RINGWOOD VIC 3134
03 9872 3400

FURNER AGENCY
UNIT 4/74 FULLARTON RD
NORWOOD SA 5067
08 8362 3968